# BIBLE · GEMS
## OF
# FAITH

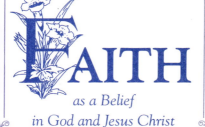

# FAITH

*as a Belief
in God and Jesus Christ*

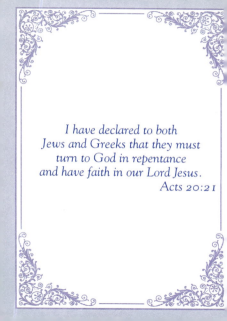

I have declared to both
Jews and Greeks that they must
turn to God in repentance
and have faith in our Lord Jesus.

Acts 20:21

*I am sending you to them*
*to open their eyes and turn them*
*from darkness to light, and from*
*the power of Satan to God, so that*
*they may receive forgiveness of*
*sins and a place among those who*
*are sanctified by faith in me.*
Acts 26:17-18

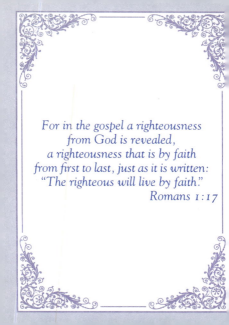

For in the gospel a righteousness
from God is revealed,
a righteousness that is by faith
from first to last, just as it is written:
"The righteous will live by faith."
Romans 1:17

*Righteousness from God
comes through faith in Jesus Christ
to all who believe.*
Romans 3:22

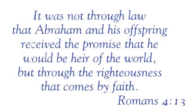

It was not through law
that Abraham and his offspring
received the promise that he
would be heir of the world,
but through the righteousness
that comes by faith.

Romans 4:13

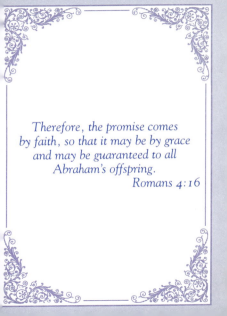

*Therefore, the promise comes
by faith, so that it may be by grace
and may be guaranteed to all
Abraham's offspring.*

Romans 4:16

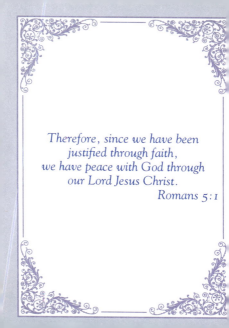

*Therefore, since we have been
justified through faith,
we have peace with God through
our Lord Jesus Christ.*

Romans 5:1

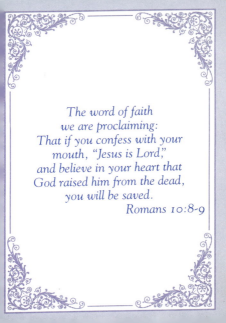

The word of faith
we are proclaiming:
That if you confess with your
mouth, "Jesus is Lord,"
and believe in your heart that
God raised him from the dead,
you will be saved.

Romans 10:8-9

*Let us draw near to God
with a sincere heart in full
assurance of faith.*
Hebrews 10:22

We are always confident
and know that as long as we
are at home in the body
we are away from the Lord.
We live by faith, not by sight.
*2 Corinthians 5:6-7*

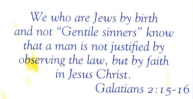

*We who are Jews by birth*
*and not "Gentile sinners" know*
*that a man is not justified by*
*observing the law, but by faith*
*in Jesus Christ.*
*Galatians 2:15-16*

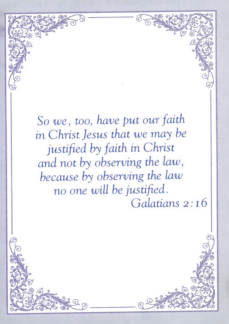

So we, too, have put our faith
in Christ Jesus that we may be
justified by faith in Christ
and not by observing the law,
because by observing the law
no one will be justified.
Galatians 2:16

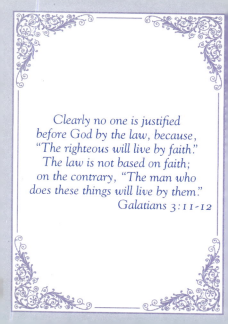

*Clearly no one is justified
before God by the law, because,
"The righteous will live by faith."
The law is not based on faith;
on the contrary, "The man who
does these things will live by them."*
*Galatians 3:11-12*

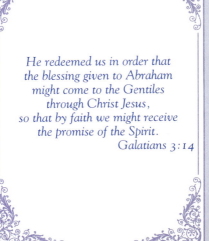

He redeemed us in order that
the blessing given to Abraham
might come to the Gentiles
through Christ Jesus,
so that by faith we might receive
the promise of the Spirit.

Galatians 3:14

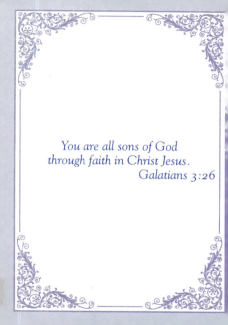

*You are all sons of God
through faith in Christ Jesus.*
*Galatians 3:26*

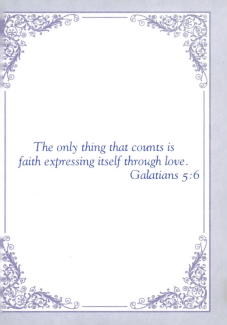

*The only thing that counts is*
*faith expressing itself through love.*
Galatians 5:6

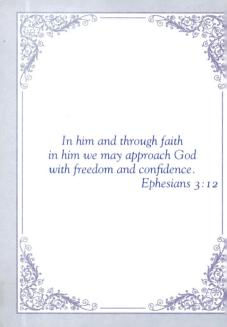

*In him and through faith
in him we may approach God
with freedom and confidence.*
*Ephesians 3:12*

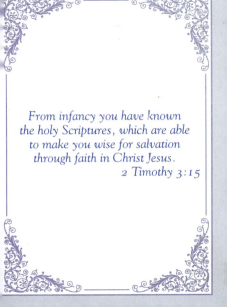

*From infancy you have known
the holy Scriptures, which are able
to make you wise for salvation
through faith in Christ Jesus.*

2 Timothy 3:15

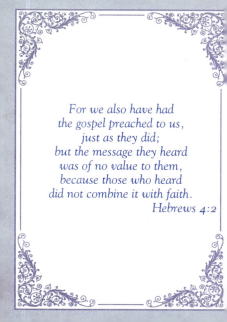

For we also have had
the gospel preached to us,
just as they did;
but the message they heard
was of no value to them,
because those who heard
did not combine it with faith.

Hebrews 4:2

*Let us hold unswervingly
to the hope we profess,
for he who promised is faithful.*
Hebrews 10:23

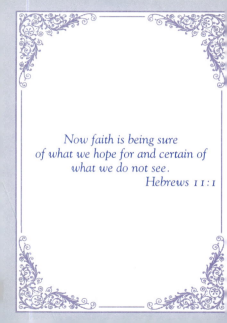

*Now faith is being sure
of what we hope for and certain of
what we do not see.*
Hebrews 11:1

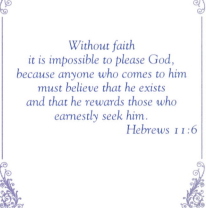

*Without faith
it is impossible to please God,
because anyone who comes to him
must believe that he exists
and that he rewards those who
earnestly seek him.*
*Hebrews 11:6*

*Let us fix our eyes on Jesus,
the author and perfecter
of our faith.*

Hebrews 12:2

*Through him you believe in God,*
*who raised him from the dead*
*and glorified him, and so your*
*faith and hope are in God.*

1 Peter 1:21

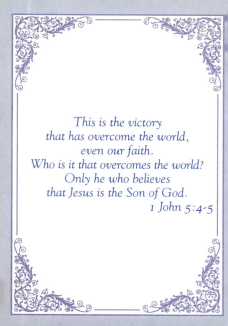

*This is the victory*
*that has overcome the world,*
*even our faith.*
*Who is it that overcomes the world?*
*Only he who believes*
*that Jesus is the Son of God.*

1 John 5:4-5

*Examples of*

# FAITH

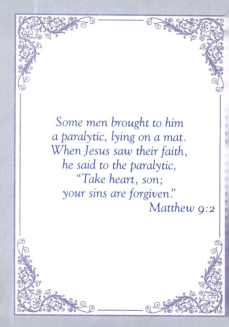

*Some men brought to him
a paralytic, lying on a mat.
When Jesus saw their faith,
he said to the paralytic,
"Take heart, son;
your sins are forgiven."*

Matthew 9:2

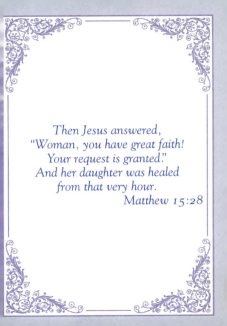

Then Jesus answered,
"Woman, you have great faith!
Your request is granted."
And her daughter was healed
from that very hour.

Matthew 15:28

*The blind man said,*
*"Rabbi, I want to see."*
*"Go," said Jesus,*
*"your faith has healed you."*
Mark 10:51-52

*By faith in the name
of Jesus, this man whom you see
and know was made strong.
It is Jesus' name and the faith that
comes through him that has given
this complete healing to him.*

Acts 3:16

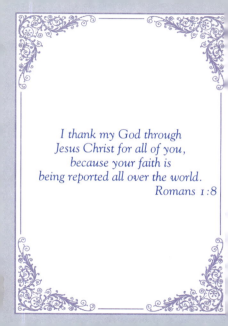

*I thank my God through
Jesus Christ for all of you,
because your faith is
being reported all over the world.*

*Romans 1:8*

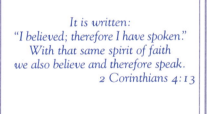

*It is written:*
*"I believed; therefore I have spoken."*
*With that same spirit of faith*
*we also believe and therefore speak.*
                              *2 Corinthians 4:13*

*We continually remember
before our God and Father your
work produced by faith.*
1 *Thessalonians* 1:3

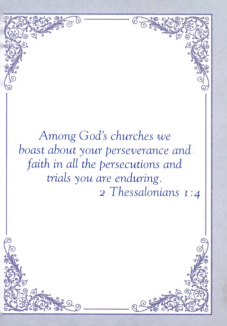

*Among God's churches we
boast about your perseverance and
faith in all the persecutions and
trials you are enduring.*

*2 Thessalonians 1:4*

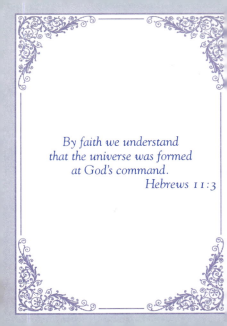

By faith we understand
that the universe was formed
at God's command.
Hebrews 11:3

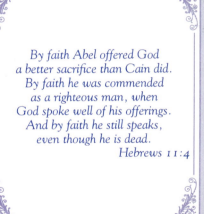

By faith Abel offered God
a better sacrifice than Cain did.
By faith he was commended
as a righteous man, when
God spoke well of his offerings.
And by faith he still speaks,
even though he is dead.

Hebrews 11:4

By faith Enoch
was taken from this life, so that
he did not experience death.
Hebrews 11:5

By faith Noah,
when warned about things
not yet seen, in holy fear built
an ark to save his family.
Hebrews 11:7

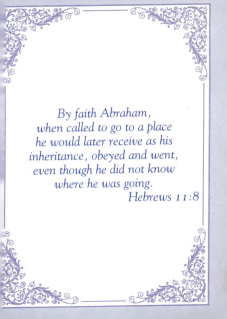

By faith Abraham,
when called to go to a place
he would later receive as his
inheritance, obeyed and went,
even though he did not know
where he was going.

Hebrews 11:8

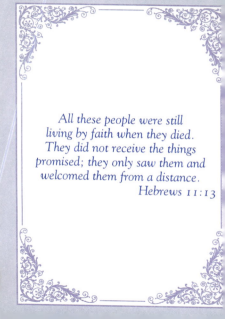

*All these people were still
living by faith when they died.
They did not receive the things
promised; they only saw them and
welcomed them from a distance.*
Hebrews 11:13

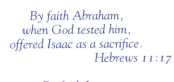

By faith Abraham,
when God tested him,
offered Isaac as a sacrifice.
*Hebrews 11:17*

By faith Isaac
blessed Jacob and Esau
in regard to their future.
*Hebrews 11:20*

By faith Moses' parents
hid him for three months
after he was born, because they
saw he was no ordinary child,
and they were not afraid of
the king's edict.

Hebrews 11:23

# FAITH

*in Action*

*Have faith in the LORD your God
and you will be upheld;
have faith in his prophets and
you will be successful.*
                    2 Chronicles 20:20

*If you do not stand firm*
*in your faith,*
*you will not stand at all.*
*Isaiah 7:9*

*Open the gates that the
righteous nation may enter,
the nation that keeps faith.*
Isaiah 26:2

See, he is puffed up;
his desires are not upright – but
the righteous will live by his faith.

*Habakkuk 2:4*

*Guard yourself in your spirit,*
*and do not break faith.*
Malachi 2:16

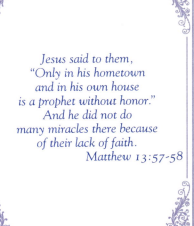

Jesus said to them,
"Only in his hometown
and in his own house
is a prophet without honor."
And he did not do
many miracles there because
of their lack of faith.
Matthew 13:57-58

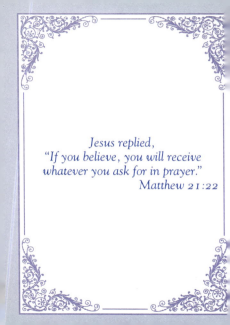

Jesus replied,
"If you believe, you will receive
whatever you ask for in prayer."
Matthew 21:22

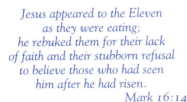

*Jesus appeared to the Eleven*
*as they were eating;*
*he rebuked them for their lack*
*of faith and their stubborn refusal*
*to believe those who had seen*
*him after he had risen.*

Mark 16:14

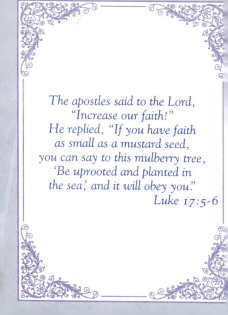

The apostles said to the Lord,
"Increase our faith!"
He replied, "If you have faith
as small as a mustard seed,
you can say to this mulberry tree,
'Be uprooted and planted in
the sea,' and it will obey you."
Luke 17:5-6

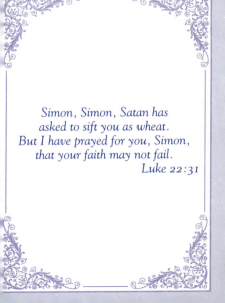

*Simon, Simon, Satan has
asked to sift you as wheat.
But I have prayed for you, Simon,
that your faith may not fail.*
Luke 22:31

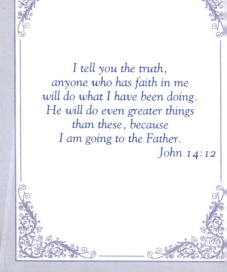

I tell you the truth,
anyone who has faith in me
will do what I have been doing.
He will do even greater things
than these, because
I am going to the Father.

John 14:12

*If I have a faith
that can move mountains,
but have not love,
I am nothing.*
1 Corinthians 13:2

Be on your guard;
stand firm in the faith;
be men of courage;
be strong.
*1 Corinthians 16:13*

Take up the shield of faith,
with which you can extinguish
all the flaming arrows
of the evil one.
Ephesians 6:16

*Since we belong to the day,
let us be self-controlled,
putting on faith and love
as a breastplate.*
　　　*1 Thessalonians 5:8*

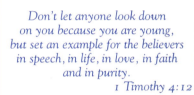

*Don't let anyone look down
on you because you are young,
but set an example for the believers
in speech, in life, in love, in faith
and in purity.*
1 Timothy 4:12

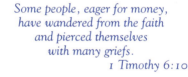

*Some people, eager for money,*
*have wandered from the faith*
*and pierced themselves*
*with many griefs.*
1 Timothy 6:10

But you, man of God,
flee from all this,
and pursue righteousness,
godliness, faith, love,
endurance and gentleness.
Fight the good fight of the faith.

*1 Timothy 6:11-12*

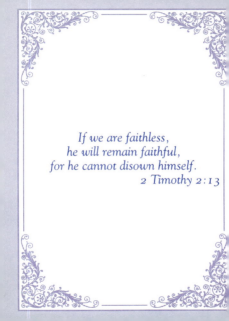

*If we are faithless,*
*he will remain faithful,*
*for he cannot disown himself.*
    *2 Timothy 2:13*

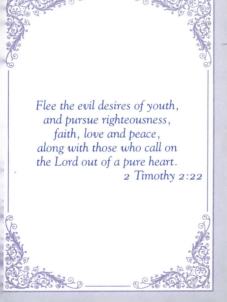

*Flee the evil desires of youth,
and pursue righteousness,
faith, love and peace,
along with those who call on
the Lord out of a pure heart.*
2 Timothy 2:22

*Teach the older men*
*to be temperate, worthy of respect,*
*self-controlled, and sound in faith,*
*in love and in endurance.*

*Titus 2:2*

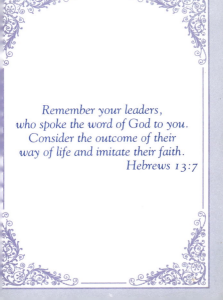

*Remember your leaders,*
*who spoke the word of God to you.*
*Consider the outcome of their*
*way of life and imitate their faith.*
*Hebrews 13:7*

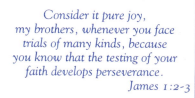

Consider it pure joy,
my brothers, whenever you face
trials of many kinds, because
you know that the testing of your
faith develops perseverance.

James 1:2-3